JAN 18

NEW ZEALAND LANDSCAPES

DEAR VIRGINIA

GREAT TO HAVE YOU IN NZ
LOOKING FORWARD TO WELCOMING
YOU BACK.

NGĀ MIHI

IRIS

NEW ZEALAND LANDSCAPES

PHOTOGRAPHY BY ANDRIS APSE

craig potton publishing

DEDICATION

To the memory of my mother Kamilla

ACKNOWLEDGEMENTS

There are many people whose generous assistance over the last twenty years has enabled me to collect thousands of images throughout New Zealand. Many of the photographs would have been difficult if not impossible to achieve without the generous assistance of the following people: Alan Bond, Richard Hayes, Tim Innes, Lou Sanson, Dave Saxton, Jeff Shanks, Ken Tustin and Simon Williamson.

PREVIOUS PAGE: Kahikatea forest in South Westland beneath Mt Tasman and Aoraki/Mt Cook (right of centre).

First published 2006 by Craig Potton Publishing
98 Vickerman Street, PO Box 555, Nelson, New Zealand
www.craigpotton.co.nz

Reprinted 2007, 2008, 2009, 2010, 2011

ISBN 1-877333-43-3
ISBN 978-1-877333-43-9

Scanning by Image Centre, Auckland, New Zealand
Printed in China by Midas Printing International Ltd

CONTENTS

For 150 years or more, writers, painters and photographers have been drawing attention to the fact that New Zealand as a whole contains a variety of landscapes and scenery unmatched anywhere else in the world, at all events, within such a compact area. In this small country have been gathered together numerous graphic examples of the great earth-shaping processes of tectonic upheaval, volcanic mayhem and massive glaciation. Coupled with factors like 80 million years of isolation from other large land areas and a frequent occurrence of climatic extremes, these processes have resulted in the highest mountains in Australasia; the most accessible glaciers in the world's temperate regions; a huge (upwards of 10,000 kilometres) and wonderfully diverse expanse of coastline; large tracts of virgin rainforest; stark areas of semi-arid terrain; and a liberal sprinkling of highly individual flourishes in things like intriguing areas of karst (or limestone) landscapes and dazzling examples of geothermal creativity. Here too dramatic contrasts abound, often in close proximity – dry eastern areas and a vastly wetter west; gentle plains terminating in abrupt mountain ranges; a subtropical north and a distinctly temperate south; and large areas of essentially untouched natural wilderness giving way, often quite abruptly, to settled landscapes from which all traces of former wildness have frequently been erased. Qualities like these – and this is by no means a comprehensive catalogue – go some way towards explaining how it is that a photographer of Andris's talents and ambition is able to find everything he needs to satisfy his artistic inclinations without feeling the necessity of travelling to distant lands.

Andy Dennis

From the introduction to the standard
edition of *New Zealand Landscapes*

George Sound, Fiordland National Park.

COASTLINE

Ninety Mile Beach, Northland.

Nugget Point lighthouse and eroded rock stacks at sunrise, Catlins Coast, South Otago.

RIGHT: Ohinemaka Beach, South Westland.
OVERLEAF: Morning cloud disperses from Milford Sound's buttresses and Mitre Peak after a southwesterly storm, Fiordland National Park.

LEFT: Lake McKerrow drains into Martins Bay, Fiordland National Park. OVERLEAF: Cape Reinga, Northland, the northernmost point of the New Zealand mainland.

ABOVE: Mitre Peak, Milford Sound, Fiordland National Park.
PREVIOUS PAGE: Breaksea Sound, Fiordland National Park.

Ocean swells erupt spectacularly through blowholes at Punakaiki in Paparoa National Park.

Storm-driven surf surges onto Penguin Beach on the Otago Peninsula.

Port Jackson and Cape Colville on the Coromandel Peninsula, with Great Barrier Island behind.

ABOVE: Hoopers Inlet and Papanui Inlet from Peggys Hill, Otago Peninsula.
OVERLEAF: Awaroa Bay, Abel Tasman National Park.

LOWLAND WILDERNESS

Coastal forest beneath the Southern Alps near Waiho, South Westland.

ABOVE: Mt Tasman and Aoraki/Mt Cook (right of centre) reflected in Okarito Lagoon.
OVERLEAF: Moss-draped ribbonwood forest and blechnum ferns at Kiwi Lake, Wild Natives Valley, Fiordland National Park.

Forest trunks and tree ferns, Breaksea Sound, Fiordland National Park.

Beech forest and ferns growing beside a stream in Preservation Inlet, Fiordland National Park.

Mouth of the Waiho River and the Southern Alps, South Westland.

Looking across the Hope Arm of Lake Manapouri, Fiordland National Park.

Mt Taranaki from the Waiwhakaiho River.

Korokoro Falls, Urewera National Park.

Small forest waterfall at the head of George Sound, Fiordland National Park.

PASTORAL LAND

Stooked oats on a North Canterbury farm.

ABOVE: Sunrise over farmland in the Geraldine area, South Canterbury.
OVERLEAF: Golden fields and river escarpment near Kyeburn, Central Otago.

Twisted and wind-shorn macrocarpa trees at Pahia on Southland's southern coast.

ABOVE: Ngaranui Station, near Carterton, Wairarapa.
OVERLEAF: The Canterbury Plains and the Rakaia River below the foothills of the Southern Alps.

RIGHT: Mudstone hill country farmland near Tahora in the Taumarunui district, King Country. PREVIOUS PAGE: Sheep flock being herded on undulating downs at 'Woodlands' near Temuka, South Canterbury.

Cape Egmont lighthouse with Mt Taranaki in the distance.

ABOVE: Vineyard on Waiheke Island.
OVERLEAF: Church, cemetery and barley crop near Taihape, Rangitikei District.

Hereford cattle grazing beneath the Southern Alps near Fox Glacier.

ABOVE: Autumn poplars and willows at Macetown, Central Otago.
PREVIOUS PAGE: Farmland near Fairlie showing the Ben McLeod Range, South Canterbury.

ABOVE: Tolaga Bay farmland, East Cape.
OVERLEAF: Bannockburn and the Pisa Range, Central Otago.

HIGH COUNTRY

Drowned willows in Lake Wanaka, Otago.

ABOVE: High-country cattle muster on Birchwood Station in the upper Dingle Burn, east of Lake Hawea, Central Otago. OVERLEAF: Tussock and fog in the Matukituki Valley, Otago, with Mt Aspiring/Tititea in the centre.

LEFT: Larch trees in autumn and the Mt Cook massif from the shores of Lake Pukaki.
OVERLEAF: Stormbound Southern Alps from the head of Lake Tekapo looking north up the Godley Valley.

RIGHT: Sunrise at Lake Onslow, east of Roxborough, in Central Otago.
PREVIOUS PAGE: Salmon fisherman in the upper Rakaia River, Canterbury.

Autumn larch trees at Castle Hill, with the Torlesse Range beyond, Canterbury.

ABOVE: The upper Ahuriri Valley after a mid-winter snowfall, Mackenzie Country.
OVERLEAF: Ben Avon Station, upper Ahuriri Valley.

ABOVE: Musterer and dogs on Dalrachney Station, near Lindis Pass, Mackenzie Country.
PREVIOUS PAGE: Lake Tekapo in the Mackenzie Country, South Canterbury.

ABOVE: Looking west across Lake Hawea towards Mt Aspiring/Tititea (obscured) and the peaks of Mount Aspiring National Park. OVERLEAF: Tussockland at Mesopotamia Station, Rangitata River, Canterbury.

MOUNTAINS

Head of the Fox Glacier, with Mt Tasman and Aoraki/Mt Cook,
Westland/Tai Poutini National Park.

A 'hogsback' storm cloud enshrouds Aoraki/Mt Cook at sunset.

Icefall on the upper Fox Glacier, with Mt Douglas and Mt Haidinger right of centre.

LEFT: The Red Hills, South Westland. OVERLEAF: Lake Wanaka and the Southern Alps from Roys Peak.

Looking down on the Route Burn flats from the Routeburn Track after a winter snowfall, Mount Aspiring National Park.

Lake Leeb above the Arawata Valley looking east to the Haast Range, South Westland.

Mt Ngauruhoe and Mt Ruapehu at sunset, Tongariro National Park.

Mt Taranaki reflected in a tarn, Egmont National Park.

Rata in flower in the Copland Valley, Westland/Tai Poutini National Park.

ABOVE: Mt Tasman (centre) and Aoraki/Mt Cook, from a ridge high above the Fox Glacier in Westland/ Tai Poutini National Park. OVERLEAF: Skiers on Fox Glacier, Westland/Tai Poutini National Park.

Mt Aspiring/Tititea and the Bonar Glacier from the southwest.

ISLANDS

Sulphur deposits and steaming fumaroles in the White Island crater, Bay of Plenty.

Steam and sulphur vapour from the White Island volcano, Bay of Plenty.

Mason Bay dunelands, Rakiura National Park, Stewart Island.

Tree on a clifftop against a stormy sky, Kahunene, Chatham Islands.

ABOVE: Sooty albatross nesting amongst megaherbs on a rock outcrop above Fly Harbour, Adams Island, Auckland Islands. PREVIOUS PAGE: Surf at West Ruggedy Beach, Rakiura National Park, Stewart Island, with Codfish Island on the right.

Wandering albatross, Adams Island, Auckland Islands.

Erect-crested penguin colony and rock stack on Antipodes Island, 1000km southeast of New Zealand.